Measuring the Tempo of the Mobility Air Forces

Tim Bonds, Dan Norton, Peter Hirneise,
Pete Ellis, Paul Killingsworth

Prepared for the United States Air Force

PROJECT AIR FORCE

The research reported here was sponsored by the United States Air Force under Contract F49642-01-C-0003. Further information may be obtained from the Strategic Planning Division, Directorate of Plans, Hq USAF.

Library of Congress Cataloging-in-Publication Data

Measuring the tempo of the mobility air forces / Tim Bonds ... [et al.].
    p. cm.
    "TR-150."
    Includes bibliographical references.
    ISBN 0-8330-3657-2 (pbk. : alk. paper)
    1. Airlift, Military—United States. 2. United States. Air Force—Operational readiness—Measurement. 3. Deployment (Strategy) I. Bonds, Tim, 1962–

UC333.M43 2005
358.4'44—dc22

2004015317

Published 2005 by the RAND Corporation
1776 Main Street, P.O. Box 2138, Santa Monica, CA 90407-2138
1200 South Hayes Street, Arlington, VA 22202-5050
201 North Craig Street, Suite 202, Pittsburgh, PA 15213-1516
RAND URL: http://www.rand.org/
To order RAND documents or to obtain additional information, contact
Distribution Services: Telephone: (310) 451-7002;
Fax: (310) 451-6915; Email: order@rand.org

Preface

The authors in this research propose a new metric for measuring the effect of operations tempo (OPTEMPO) on the readiness of the mobility air forces (MAF). The research should be of interest to Air Force and Department of Defense leaders and planners charged with managing the MAF.

The research documented in this report was conducted during fiscal years 2001, 2002, and 2003 as part of a project entitled "Addressing the Peacetime Tempo of the Mobility Air Forces." This report supplements the main report from that study, *The Peacetime Tempo of Air Mobility Operations: Meeting Demand and Maintaining Readiness*, MR-1506-AF, by Brian Chow. A related report, *Designing Transload Concepts of Operations for the Civil Reserve Air Fleet to Respond to North Korean Chemical and Biological Threats*, was published in 2002 (Government report; not for public release). The project was sponsored by the Commander, Air Mobility Command, and was conducted as part of the Aerospace Force Development Program of RAND Project AIR FORCE.

RAND Project AIR FORCE

RAND Project AIR FORCE (PAF), a division of the RAND Corporation, is the U.S. Air Force's federally funded research and development center for studies and analysis. PAF provides the Air Force with independent analyses of policy alternatives affecting the development, employment, combat readiness, and support of current and future aerospace forces. Research is performed in four programs: Aerospace Force Development; Manpower, Personnel, and Training; Resource Management; and Strategy and Doctrine.

Additional information about PAF is available on our web site at http://www.rand.org/paf.

Contents

Figures

Tables

Summary

The analysis described in this report suggests a new metric—the mission-day—to identify and examine the ability of the mobility air forces (MAF) to conduct missions, train its forces, and maintain readiness for new operations. Specifically, the mission-day metric can help the MAF detect and identify problems caused by the operations tempo (OPTEMPO) of MAF personnel.

The mobility OPTEMPO is driven primarily by two categories of missions. The first category is missions that involve maintaining readiness to accomplish the tasks demanded of the mobility forces during major theater operations. These tasks include the delivery of troops and material to combat theaters, providing tanker support to mobility and combat aircraft in transit, and performing other specialized missions such as dropping paratroops. The second category of mobility missions is support of U.S. forces engaged in peacetime operations around the world. These include the support of small-scale contingencies (SSCs), humanitarian relief operations (HUMROs), presidential travel (called BANNERs), and other short-notice and high-priority missions flown on a daily basis (see Chapter 2).

Historically, the air mobility force is resourced to stay ready for war. Peacetime operations have been supported as a "by-product" of the MAF training for war. During the 1990s, however, there was some concern among the military leadership that the tempo of peacetime engagement missions had become too burdensome on the MAF crews and had started to interfere with maintaining wartime readiness (see Chapter 3). In fact, the MAF has proven able to meet the demands of Operation Enduring Freedom and Operation Iraqi Freedom.

When mobility operations in support of Operation Enduring Freedom and Operation Iraqi Freedom eventually wind down, the MAF will go through a period in which any deferred education, training, and personnel rotations will need to be addressed. Also, pilots who have remained in the service may take the opportunity to leave once these wars have ended.

The Air Force will need to monitor the effects of these factors on MAF capabilities to ensure that the capabilities are in balance with the operational demands placed on the MAF. What we have found lacking in previous discussions is a way to quantify the workload and OPTEMPO stresses being placed on the MAF (see Chapter 4). Therefore, we developed the **mission-day** metric, which measures the availability of crewmembers to fly missions while continuing needed training and other activities. It is essentially a person-day analysis of the capacity of the mobility air forces to fly missions, continue essential training, and conduct other activities during peace or war (see Chapter 5).

In this report we describe this metric, apply it to one exemplar airlift wing, and discuss how it might be used in the future by the Air Force to plan operations at the major command and unit levels and to identify OPTEMPO problems.

Abbreviations and Acronyms

ACP	Aircrew Continuation Pay
AFB	Air Force Base
AFORMS	Air Force Operational Readiness Management System
AFPD	Air Force Personnel Data System
AMC	Air Mobility Command
AMW	Air Mobility Wing
BANNER	Presidential Support Mission
CCR	Cumulative Continuation Rate
GDSS	Global Decision Support System
HUMRO	Humanitarian Relief Operation
JA/ATT	Joint Airborne/Air Transportability Training
LM	Load Master
MAF	Mobility Air Forces
MAJCOM	Major Command
MTM/Day	Million Ton-Miles per Day
OEF	Operation Enduring Freedom
OIF	Operation Iraqi Freedom
OPTEMPO	Operations Tempo
PCS	Permanent Change of Station
SAAM	Special Assignment Airlift Mission
SOLL	Special Operations Low Level
SSC	Small-Scale Contingency
TDY	Temporary Duty
TEMPO	Characteristic pace of activity within a given unit
VIP	Very Important Person

1. Introduction

The operational tempo of our mobility air forces (MAF) has been a subject of continuing concern for the Air Mobility Command (AMC). OPTEMPO, short for operations tempo, is a term used to describe the pace of military operations. Military forces that are busy are said to have high OPTEMPO. Senior officers at MAF wings and AMC have often expressed concern that the demands on the MAF to support peacetime missions and perform additional duties were too high. The OPTEMPO was making it difficult to maintain readiness for major wars and maintain a reasonable quality of life for aircrew members.

Some evidence existed before September 11, 2001, that the stresses on the MAF were causing pilots to separate at an increasing rate. These stresses included high OPTEMPO, additional duties, and time away from home station (or TDY rate) and will be discussed in Chapter 2. The attacks of September 11, the subsequent Global War On Terror, and the war in Iraq have dramatically changed the operations and activities of all service personnel. These events also have likely caused many service personnel, including pilots, to remain in the service longer. In addition, the financial problems of several major airlines and the extension of service member duty tours (known as "Stop Loss") have limited opportunities for pilots outside of the service. However, the airlines will begin hiring pilots again at some point, creating new civilian opportunities for military pilots.

The Air Force needs tools and metrics to understand the stresses placed on the mobility air forces so that training, OPTEMPO, and other demands can be managed appropriately. Unfortunately, as we will describe in Chapter 3 of this report, metrics currently used by the Air Force do not provide an easy way to predict, detect, or identify stresses or their causes. What the Air Force needs is a metric that accounts for the workload demands placed upon the MAF and compares them to the supply of MAF aircrew members. We discuss such a new metric, termed the **mission-day.** The mission-day metric can highlight periods of stress and illuminate the potential effectiveness of alternative solutions. Although we concentrate in this report on the mobility air forces in our examples, the mission-day metric should be equally applicable to combat air forces as well.

2. The Operational Tempo of the Mobility Air Forces

Categories of Mobility Missions

The types of missions flown by the mobility air forces in recent years are shown in Figure 2.1. Missions in the upper half of the figure are often conducted on short notice. We term these engagement missions because they typically are conducted in support of high-priority diplomatic and military missions short of major theater wars. These missions include special assignment air missions (SAAMs), the delivery of peacekeeping forces and humanitarian relief (HUMRO), transportation of the President and other senior U.S. officials (BANNER missions), support of military operations in small-scale contingencies (SSCs), and participation in a myriad of small and large regional exercises with other militaries.

Missions in the lower half of the figure are typically scheduled in advance. We term these readiness missions because their main utility is training MAF aircrews and preparing the MAF to conduct wartime operations. Readiness missions

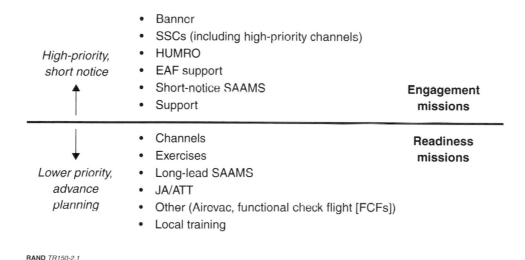

RAND *TR150-2.1*

Figure 2.1—Engagement Missions vs. Readiness Missions

include channels (flights supporting the logistical needs of deployed forces), exercises, long-notice SAAMs, specialized training (such as Joint Airborne Air Transportability Training or JA/ATT), and local training.

Maintaining Readiness for War

In peacetime, the mobility force structure conducts training missions to maintain the readiness needed to execute wartime missions. For the active force, ready forces must be "grown" from scratch. Large numbers of aircrew, maintenance, and support personnel must be brought from an unqualified status up through progressively higher levels of qualification to yield experts in each area. This training is programmed and budgeted in terms of a flying-hour program, which funds annual flying hours for each aircraft type. The program represents the minimum flying time needed to keep the crews trained and developing their experience and skills. The hours in the flying-hour program, which exists to train crews, also create a peacetime transportation capacity that is allocated among peacetime demands. This capacity is available in peacetime to support engagement missions and other mobility needs.

The wartime readiness of an active duty MAF unit is sustained by activities beyond honing specialized flying skills to conduct wartime missions. Crewmembers receive broad career, leadership, and management training to advance their careers and future worth to the Air Force. Airmen receive this training by attending service schools (e.g., Squadron Officer School, Non-Commissioned Officer Academy) and by taking correspondence courses. Crewmembers also receive training in general military skills that are peripheral to their primary duties, such as small arms, chemical warfare defense, and water survival training. In addition, airmen are tasked to help administer their squadrons, groups, and wings by performing a wide range of duties as schedulers, training officers, command-post duty officers, and so on.[1] Ideally, quality-of-life issues of the members throughout the lengthy process are taken into account—to aid in retention, thereby sustaining readiness through the long term.

During a major theater war, the activities that maintain readiness are placed on hold. All efforts are focused on deploying troops and equipment in support of a combatant commander's warplan. When the crisis subsides, a period of

---

[1] These activities serve the dual purpose of holding down unit administrative costs and providing crewmembers with the broader leadership and management experience required to advance in their careers.

reconstitution ensues during which the deferred activities are conducted to recover readiness for the wartime mission.

Peacetime Engagement

Normal readiness training in peacetime gives the MAF a certain ability in peacetime to support engagement missions and still maintain wartime readiness. Over the last decade, the MAF has been engaged in supporting U.S. peacetime security strategy on a daily basis. Tankers and airlifters are among the forces most frequently used to support peacetime operations, which are typically high-priority and short-notice.

To some degree, small-scale contingencies, presidential support missions, humanitarian relief operations, and so on, fall into the usual business areas of exercises, channels, special assignment airlift missions. However, while the top line of the flying-hour program is rarely exceeded, these engagement activities have in some years taken up a significant portion of the total flying-hour program. Too many short-notice missions can interfere with needed training activities or place too great a strain on aircrew members. On the other hand, if too many short-notice missions are given to commercial carriers, then the funds paid to those commercial carriers are not being used to support missions suitable for readiness training, with the result that some training events are forgone or are performed inefficiently.

It is unclear what demands will be placed on the mobility air forces over the next decade by (a) force rotations in Iraq and Afghanistan, (b) operations against terror groups, and (c) exercises with coalition partners. The MAF must carefully monitor its ability to provide the needed support to these operations while maintaining readiness to conduct other operations. Although pilots are choosing to stay in the service at present, they may choose to leave in the future once the current wars have ended. It is therefore important to have adequate metrics with which to monitor the ability of the MAF to conduct current operations, train and educate its personnel, and maintain readiness to conduct new operations.

Before turning to the topic of metrics, we discuss whether signs of strain on the MAF can be detected and if the activities and stresses that cause this strain can be identified. Any metrics that we develop must be carefully designed and calibrated to detect and measure these strains. In the next chapter, we identify areas of stress that emerged before the Global War on Terror began.

3. Identifying Stresses on the Mobility Air Forces

Prior to operations in Afghanistan and Iraq, the adverse effects of "too much" peacetime OPTEMPO were reported by rated officers at the wing and major command (MAJCOM) levels. For example, we received reports in the late 1990s that the number of missions to support VIP travel and short-notice missions had greatly increased. If the mobility forces have been asked to perform an increasingly demanding workload, we would expect to see some effect on the quality of training, on retention, or on quality-of-life satisfaction.[1]

However, it is difficult to determine from available command data exactly when excessive demands were placed upon MAF aircrews, precisely what those demands were, when the stresses that they caused were at their peak, and which units were most affected. We examined aircrew retention statistics and quality-of-life surveys for empirical data to help pinpoint specific sources of stress for MAF aircrew members. Then we developed metrics to help the Air Force track these stresses and determine when and for which units the stresses had reached unacceptable levels.

We first looked at aircrew retention statistics prior to September 11, 2001.[2] Table 3.1 depicts the cumulative continuation rate (CCR) time series for all pilots and navigators in the Air Force through FY 2000.

Through the end of FY 2000, we found evidence that flight crew retention, as measured by the cumulative continuation rate, had experienced a steady decline. Cumulative continuation rates refer to the cumulative numbers of people of a particular cohort (such as those with 6–11 years of service in the Air Force) who decide to stay in the Air Force rather than separate. In these time series, the CCR for all Air Force pilots in the 6–11 year cohorts fell from 87 percent in FY 1995 to

---

[1] Brian Chow found that training suffered immediately after the Kosovo conflict for two reasons: First, the average number of pilots onboard per flight had been increasing. The AMC rule had been to give each pilot on board credit toward his or her "aging" requirements, regardless of whether the pilot was in the pilot seat for the entire flight or not. More pilots on board each flight meant that each pilot received less in-seat training. Second, AMC airlifters flew fewer hours than programmed, resulting in insufficient flying hours to meet requirements. See Brian Chow (2003).

[2] Aircrew retention data obtained from Headquarters, U.S. Air Force, Office of the Deputy Chief of Staff for Personnel, September 2001.

Table 3.1

Cumulative Continuation Rate (CCR)

	FY95	FY96	FY97	FY98	FY99	FY00
Pilot (6–14 CCR)	87%	77%	71%	46%	41%	45%
Navigator (6–14 CCR)	86%	75%	73%	62%	62%	69%
NROs[a] (4–11 CCR)	54%	62%	59%	57%	56%	51%

[a] Nonrated officers.

45 percent in FY 2000, with a low of 41 percent in FY 1999. Navigator CCRs for the 6–11 year cohort fell from 86 percent in FY 1995 to 69 percent in FY 2000, with a low of 62 percent in 1999. The CCRs for NROs held a bit steadier, declining from 62 percent in FY 1996 to 51 percent in FY 2000.

We also obtained data regarding the percentage of Air Mobility Command aircrew personnel who chose to accept aircrew continuation pay (ACP) bonuses to remain in the Air Force for another tour (Table 3.2). Continuation pay acceptances have declined in the Air Mobility Command, from 66 percent in FY 1995 to 34 percent in FY 2000, with a low of 19 percent in FY 1998. For the Air Force as a whole, ACP acceptances have declined from 76 percent in FY 1995 to 39 percent in FY 2000, with a low of 27 percent in FY 1998.

These data strongly suggest that pilots as a whole had been leaving the service in increasing numbers through the end of FY 2000. Moreover, it suggests that the same was not true of NROs, who had been retained at a fairly steady rate during the period shown. However, it is notable that the retention of navigators exceeded that of pilots, perhaps because fewer job opportunities existed for

Table 3.2

Aircrew Continuation Pay (ACP) Acceptances
(in percentages)

Year	Air Mobility Command	Total Air Force
FY95	66	76
FY96	49	58
FY97	24	34
FY98	19	27
FY99	34	42
FY00	34	39

navigators in the commercial airline industry. Comparisons between aviators and non-aviators are complicated by differing initial opportunities to separate. Non-aviators have an initial opportunity to separate after four years, whereas aviators had to remain for six years before they could separate.[3]

Of course, simply noting a decline in retention does not indicate the cause. By itself, retention data do not indicate whether personnel are leaving the Air Force because of a reduced quality of life or if that reduced quality of life is the direct, or sole, result of increased OPTEMPO. It might be that personnel left the Air Force to pursue higher-paying jobs in private industry, or perhaps for this reason in concert with other influences.[4] It is difficult to ascribe direct cause-and-effect relationships based on the multiple, corollary datasets presented here. To infer a cause, we need to evaluate the reasons for early separations. To do so, we assessed the *Report on Career Decisions in the Air Force,* which surveyed Air Force personnel to determine reasons that they separated between FY 1996 and FY 2000.[5]

The responses collected for this study were obtained from personnel deciding to remain in the Air Force, from personnel deciding to leave for jobs in private industry, and from personnel who were undecided about making the Air Force a career. Data for these groups were broken down into pilots and all others, and by company-grade and field-grade officer ranks. In the FY 2000 report, the most pertinent information concerned motivations for leaving the service. The top 20 such reasons were listed for each group of officers.

Field-grade pilots left for a variety of reasons, as shown in Table 3.3. It is notable that three of the top seven reasons include some measure of individual workload: the number of additional duties performed by each individual; the home-station OPTEMPO of each individual; and the number of TDY days away from the home station of each individual.

By comparison, additional duties were twenty-first out of twenty-six concerns reported for field-grade officers who are not pilots. Tempo away from home (TDY) and home-station OPTEMPO were numbers 7 and 4, respectively, of the top twenty-six concerns for field-grade nonpilots.

---

[3] Beginning with graduating pilots in FY 2002, aviators must now remain for 10 years before they can separate.

[4] In fact, data in Hamilton and Datko (2000) suggest that availability of comparable civilian jobs consistently ranks toward the top "influences to leave" for all officer and enlisted personnel.

[5] See Hamilton and Datko (2000).

Table 3.3

Officer Influences to Leave—Field-Grade Pilots
(percentage surveyed who name this item as one reason for separating)

Field-Grade Pilots	2000 n=38 "Very Strong" or "Strong" Influence [Rank/% of 38 Items]	1999 n=51 "Very Strong" or "Strong" Influence [Rank/% of 28 Items]
Choice of job assignment	1/74	2/53
Availability of comparable civilian jobs	2/71	1/59
Amount of additional duties	3/55	5/47
Say in base assignment	4/53	4/51
Home station TEMPO (work schedule)	5/47	9/41
Number of PCS[a] moves	6/47	7/45
TEMPO away (number/duration of TDYs)	7/39	8/43
Availability of dependent medical care	8/37	11/37
Leadership at wing or equivalent level	9/34	10/41
Leadership at MAJCOM/HQ USAF level	10/32	3/51

[a]Permanent change of station.

By comparison, additional duties were twenty-first out of twenty-six concerns reported for field-grade officers who are not pilots. Tempo away from home (TDY) and home-station OPTEMPO were numbers 7 and 4, respectively, of the top twenty-six concerns for field-grade nonpilots.

For company-grade officer pilots, the quality-of-life results are even more striking (Table 3.4). Additional duties were the top reason for these officers leaving the Air Force. Home-station OPTEMPO and TDY days were the third and sixth leading reasons for separating. This compares to tenth place for additional duties, thirteenth place for TDY, and seventeenth place for home-station TEMPO for company-grade nonpilots.

Although the data in Table 3.4 are somewhat fragmentary, they do provide the following insights. First, pilot retention rates within the Air Force had been declining prior to Operation Enduring Freedom.[6] Furthermore, the retention

---

[6] Recent financial problems have caused most major airlines to reduce the number of scheduled flights and the numbers of pilots that they employ. New hiring of airline pilots appears to have been largely curtailed—at least temporarily. In addition, a higher percentage of military personnel choose to extend their service commitments during times of war. The current lack of job opportunities in the commercial sector as well as extended service commitments should relieve retention problems in the near term. In the long term, these conditions may be reversed.

Table 3.4

Officer Influences to Leave—Company-Grade Pilots

Company-Grade Pilots	2000 n=53 "Very Strong" or "Strong" Influence [Rank/% of 38 Items]	1999 n=98 "Very Strong" or "Strong" Influence [Rank/% of 28 Items]	1996 n=26 "Very Strong" or "Strong" Influence [Rank/% of 23 Items]
Amount of additional duties	1/75	5/66	4/46
Availability of comparable civilian jobs	2/68	4/68	4/46
Home-station TEMPO (work schedule)	3/64	9/45	11/23
Choice of job assignment	4/62	2/69	1/54
Say in base assignment	5/60	3/69	3/54
TEMPO away (number/duration of TDYs)	6/55	7/48	2/54
Retirement program that affects you	7/45	1/70	9/27
Leadership at MAJCOM/HQ USAF level	8/38	6/60	6/39
Availability of dependent medical care	9/38	10/44	8/27
Number of PCS moves	10/38	11/38	14/16

rate of AMC aircrews appears to have been lower than that of all Air Force aircrews. While we do not know the reason(s) for all of this decline, we do know that both company-grade and field-grade pilots note additional duties, home station OPTEMPO, and temporary duty away from home as leading reasons for separating from the Air Force.

The effect was more pronounced for company-grade pilots than for field-grade pilots. Both company-grade and field-grade pilots listed these reasons as more compelling for leaving than did their nonpilot peers. Additionally, the three tempo-related reasons for separating had risen in their relative ranking among "influences to leave" over the last few years for pilots in general.[7] Data from these surveys also indicate that Air Force personnel tended to follow through on their stated career intentions. Further, over half of separating personnel made the decision to do so more than one year in advance, and they were unlikely to change their minds after making this decision.[8]

---

[7] Hamilton and Datko (2000).

[8] Ibid., p. 16.

We suspect that these trends have largely been arrested since September 11, 2001, for several reasons. First, many military members may have elected to remain in the service to support the nation in a time of great need. In addition, Stop Loss—a program to involuntarily extend the tours of duty for service members possessing critical skills—was implemented in late 2001 and again in 2003. Finally, fewer commercial aviation opportunities exist today as a result of the poor financial health of the airline industry. However, the stresses identified may again lead large numbers of pilots to separate from the Air Force if the nation returns to a time of relative peace.

4. Existing Metrics for Measuring OPTEMPO

After finding specific evidence of stresses upon the MAF aircrews, we assessed existing metrics to determine whether they provided any means of detecting and identifying these stresses before there was a negative effect on readiness. We started by examining the metrics already used by AMC to measure MAF readiness:

- Million ton-miles/day
- Flying-hour program execution
- Currency training accomplishment
- Upgrade training accomplishment
- TDY days per crewmember per year

Million Ton-Miles/Day

Millions of ton miles/day, or MTM/day, is a high-level measure of the capacity of the MAF to accomplish its wartime mission. Each active and reserve MAF unit and Civil Reserve Air Fleet (CRAF) component contributes a share of MTM/day capability, which is broken down by cargo type such as bulk, oversized, and outsized cargo.

Millions of ton-miles per day is an important aggregate metric for gauging force structure needs and for expressing the overall capability of the current force to support the combatant commanders' warplans. However, MTM/day has limited applicability for measuring day-to-day activity. It does not capture stresses on the system such as diverse and geographically scattered SSCs, large month-to-month OPTEMPO variances, and such items as postponed training or the quality-of-life concerns of crewmembers.

Flying-Hour Program Execution

Another quantitative measure of peacetime activity is the accomplishment of the annual flying-hour program. If the MAF is flying more than the planned number of flying hours each year, this would indicate an increase in OPTEMPO.

However, the planned flying hour levels are rarely exceeded, even in those years experiencing large contingencies and deployments. In fact, in portions of the MAF—such as the units flying the C-5—there have recently been periods in which it has been difficult to accomplish all of the programmed flying hours.

Unfortunately, flying hours alone do not capture everything that mobility personnel are actually doing, such as the additional duties noted in Chapter 3. In addition, the number of hours flown in a month can vary considerably from month to month. Greater variability reduces the efficiency with which MAF personnel are able to accomplish their various tasks and duties.

Training Accomplishment

Maintaining current crew qualifications as well as upgrading crewmembers to higher qualification levels should also offer a useful indicator of OPTEMPO. Adverse effects of OPTEMPO would be indicated to the extent that peacetime mission demands result in an observable loss or delay of training. At the unit level, we have heard anecdotes of degraded quality of training due to high OPTEMPO. In addition, other research points to potential problems with training quality.[1]

However, training is so important to the maintenance of wartime readiness that commanders will make it a high unit priority to accomplish training—further increasing the workload for crewmembers despite heavy outside obligations. Typically, training accomplishment is reported as staying "in the green."

TDY Days per Crewmember per Year

Another often-used indicator of peacetime activity is TDY days per crewmember per annum. This metric provides the average number of days per year that crewmembers are away from their home station. While it is useful for gauging and managing the stresses on personnel, it does not directly say anything about the effects of this activity on current or future wartime readiness. Additionally, tracking TDY days does not help in identifying a limit beyond which more crews or other resources are needed if wartime readiness is to be maintained.

---

[1] See Chow (2003). This research reports that more crewmembers are, on average, being assigned to a given flight. One result of this "enhanced crewing" is that crewmembers may be receiving less "seat time" for their hours flown.

5. The Mission-Day Metric and Availability for Peacetime Missions

After surveying the metrics currently being used by AMC to measure and manage MAF activity, we concluded that none of those metrics were designed to incorporate the effects on wartime readiness or peacetime flexibility of requirements or activities that may be unproductive from a training standpoint. What is needed is a metric that is useful for measuring ongoing activity—one that can directly relate that activity to maintaining wartime readiness. Such a metric must be able to measure the activity necessary to stay ready for the wartime mission, the flying hours associated with peacetime engagement, and the other duties given to aircrew members.

Specifically, we sought to determine whether there were "enough hours in the day" for AMC personnel to accomplish all of the peacetime engagement missions assigned to them, complete their training requirements to maintain readiness, and maintain an acceptable quality of life.

Definition of a Mission-Day

We developed the mission-day metric to yield an available *capacity* to fly peacetime missions and perform other duties without interference with wartime readiness. If this capacity is exceeded, then either more resources are needed to support the ongoing engagement strategy, or support to peacetime engagement missions and other duties would need to be curtailed to maintain wartime readiness.

A mission-day is basically a person-day of work. It can be summarized as a day of availability for flying peacetime missions after accounting for activities to sustain wartime readiness and quality of life. Wartime readiness activities include local flying training, ground training, additional duties, and professional development courses. Mission-days can be considered a pool of availability for flying peacetime missions without interfering with wartime readiness.

Figure 5.1 illustrates how we calculated peacetime availability to fly operational missions for a specific AMC flying wing or group. The mission-day approach started with the number of authorized or assigned crewmembers by crew position multiplied by the number of days in a month. We then made quality-of-

16

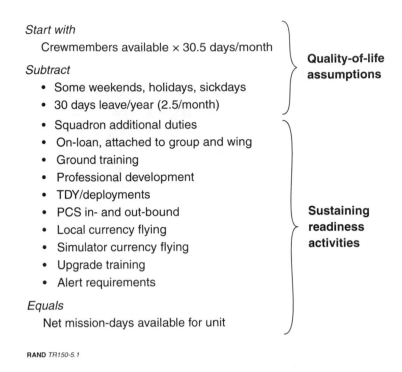

Start with
    Crewmembers available × 30.5 days/month

Subtract
  • Some weekends, holidays, sickdays
  • 30 days leave/year (2.5/month)

⎱ Quality-of-life assumptions

  • Squadron additional duties
  • On-loan, attached to group and wing
  • Ground training
  • Professional development
  • TDY/deployments
  • PCS in- and out-bound
  • Local currency flying
  • Simulator currency flying
  • Upgrade training
  • Alert requirements

⎱ Sustaining readiness activities

Equals
    Net mission-days available for unit

RAND TR150-5.1

Figure 5.1—Using Mission-Days to Calculate Availability

life assumptions based on unit practices. For example, we assumed that half of the weekends each month would be protected, with no duties assigned. Note that aircrews are usually provided an additional leave day for every three days that they are away on missions, which tends to offset the loss of some weekend days. Next we gathered data from the MAF wings on additional duties and wing- and group-level duty details. These include squadron additional duties (e.g., flying scheduler, duty officer), wing and group "on-loan" crewmembers (e.g., current operations, wing standards/evaluation, executive officer), and ancillary duties (census representative, tax advisor). We also read the training regulations[1] and estimated the number of person-days per month for each crew position that need to be dedicated to ground training, simulator training, local flying training, service schools, and so forth. Ground training requirements include tactics, small arms, flight physical, and water survival. The times required for these activities were derived from the applicable training

---

[1] See Air Mobility Command, Mobility Force Management, AMC Instruction 11-206, *Flying Operations,* 1 June 1999; Air Force Instruction 11-2C-17, Volume 1, *Flying Operations—C-17 Aircrew Training,* 1 February 1999; and Air Force Instruction 11-2C-5, Volume 1, *Flying Operations—C-5 Aircrew Training,* 1 January 1999.

regulations, and we assumed that they were spread out evenly throughout the year in order to maintain a minimum sustained level.[2]

Time away from home station, including time spent at Altus Air Force Base and attending service schools for professional development, was also estimated based on discussions with AMC training personnel, as were requirements for non-flying TDYs such as ground-mission commander duties. The requirements for local flying and simulator currency training were gleaned from training regulations, as were the requirements for the upgrade of crewmembers to higher qualification levels (e.g., qualification of first pilots as aircraft commanders, upgrade of instructor pilots to flight examiners, etc.). Much of this training is intended to take place on international missions.[3] Finally, we included alert requirements such as SOLL II and wing BRAVO alerts, but not alerts to support BANNER missions. The BANNER missions were counted later, on the requirements side of the equation.

The result of this process was a bottom-line estimate of the number of days per month needed by the aggregate crewmember population to stay ready for the wartime mission. If there are mission-days left in the month to support additional requirements, they can be available for executing the peacetime engagement mission and do not interfere with readiness for the wartime mission.

Using Mission-Days to Measure Peacetime Engagement Requirements

After calculating the objective capacity of active-duty wings and groups to support peacetime operational missions, the next step was to compare this capacity with the historical demand to support these types of missions. We developed a database of MAF missions since 1994, based on data from the AMC command-and-control system.[4] Knowing the length of each mission in days away from home station and the requirements for pre- and post-mission crew-

---

[2] For example, if crewmembers must complete water survival training every three years, we assume that 1/36th of the unit personnel takes this training each month. We believe that for most types of training, spreading out the sustaining requirement represents an objective minimum level of activity to maintain readiness. For our analysis, it results in a conservatively low estimate of monthly mission-days required to support readiness activity.

[3] Later, when we calculated the capacity of the units to support peacetime engagement missions, global missions needed for training were credited as being available at the same time that they supported wartime readiness. However, the capacity to support peacetime engagement operations was not limited to the global training missions.

[4] The data were derived from the Global Decision Support System (GDSS) used by AMC to manage the day-to-day operations of the MAF.

rest, we made the assumptions illustrated in the below equation about the crew complement required to support each peacetime engagement mission.

Begin with basic crew complement

Add another alert crew if a BANNER mission

Add another first pilot and load master x (mission length in days + pre-mission crew-rest + post-mission crew-rest) if an aerial refueling mission or if the mission has a leg longer than eight hours

Equals mission-day crew requirements

Referring to the applicable regulations, we assumed that the basic minimum crew complement would be on the airplane. The exceptions to this assumption were for BANNER missions and missions with a long leg or an aerial refueling leg.

For BANNER missions, we added a single backup alert crew, even though wings reported that two alert aircraft with their crews were often assigned to support these missions. We also added another pilot and load master to missions with an eight-hour or aerial refueling leg. This augmented crew is in accordance with AMC operating policy. We also included additional crew members for certain training missions, in accordance with AMC operating policy. This yielded an estimate, by crew position, of the mission-days expended in support of peacetime operational engagement missions each month since 1994. By comparing this historical activity with our calculations of mission-day availability, based on historical manning levels, we were able to observe as a time series the relationship between the supply and demand of mission-days in recent years.

Example: Supply and Demand of Mission-Days for the 437th Airlift Wing

As an example, we applied the mission-day metric to the units operating the C-17. The results for the 437th Airlift Wing are shown in Figure 5.2. It should be noted that these results apply only to the 437th Airlift Wing and are not indicative of the Air Force as a whole.[5] The appendix contains more details regarding the manning of C-17 units.

---

[5] The C-17 is a particularly interesting case. During the period examined, a second operational unit, the 62nd Airlift Wing, was built and equipped with the C-17. This caused some of the pilots to be transferred from the 437th to the 62nd, along with some of the mission assignments. This situation explains the decline in mission-day supply from 1999 to 2003, and accounts for the OEF and OIF demand not being higher.

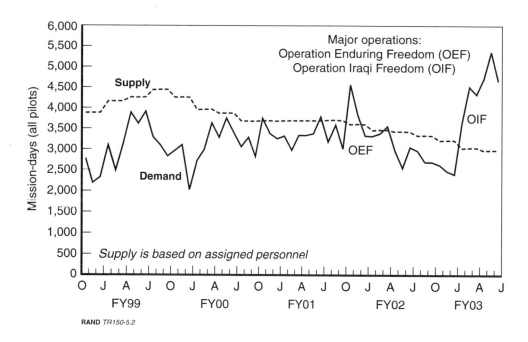

RAND *TR150-5.2*

Figure 5.2—437th AMW (C-17) Mission-Days for All Pilots

The supply and demand for mission-days for all of the 437th pilots are shown in Figure 5.2.[6] The number of available mission-days changes with the numbers of aircraft and crew assigned, while requirements tend to rise and fall according to world events. Demand spikes in the middle of FY 1999 in response to the preparation and execution of Operation Allied Force. This is followed by a reconstitution period late the following year in which demand dips significantly. Demand then increases to a relatively stable level in FY 2000, spiking again in early FY 2002 in the preparation and execution of Operation Enduring Freedom (OEF). A reconstitution period follows late the next year. Demand then increases with the deployments for Operation Iraqi Freedom (OIF) and have continued after the end of major combat operations.

The months in which demand exceeded supply are relatively few in this time frame. However, the aggregate supply-and-demand curves do not tell the whole story, since not every pilot can perform every assignment. Assignments such as aircraft command, flight instruction and evaluations, certain mission types, and

---

[6] The person-day supply calculations for FY 1999–FY 2003 were generated based on assigned personnel counts for the end of each year from the Air Force Personnel Data System (AFPDS). We noted that the AFPDS data recorded no instructor pilots or flight examiner pilots in the 437th. We assumed that these grades were all included in the aircraft commander counts. We also noted that the number of pilots shown in the AFPDS data was considerably lower than that shown in AMC's Training Review Process data for FY 2002. The mission-day demand was calculated based on actual missions flown, as reported in AMC's Global Decision Support System.

several staff positions require additional qualifications and experience. Less-experienced pilots cannot perform these functions. Although additional junior pilots can be trained relatively quickly, developing senior pilots with advanced qualifications takes several years. To understand the stresses on the more-experienced pilots (aircraft commanders and above) we plotted the supply-and-demand for them alone for the same period (see Figure 5.3).

Figure 5.3 suggests that senior pilots have been under more stress than have pilots as a whole. While demand exceeded supply only for a few months for pilots as a whole, demand for senior pilots exceeded supply for most of the four-year period we examined. The shortfalls appear to have gotten worse in FY 2002 and FY 2003, driven largely by the decline in mission-day supply. As we noted in regard to Figure 5.2, we found problems in the personnel data source for this period; for this reason, caution is warranted in interpreting the results.

This example suggests that the shortfall in mission-days is concentrated among senior pilots and that any efforts to resolve the shortfall should focus on them.

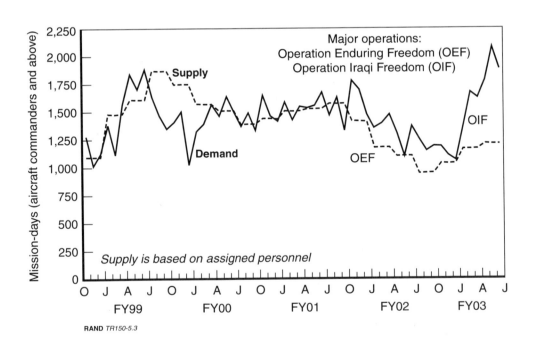

RAND TR150-5.3

Figure 5.3—437th AMW (C-17) Mission-Days for Aircraft Commanders and Above

Potential Uses of the Mission-Day Metric

The mission-day can help the Air Force improve its forecasting of demand and supply, planning of unit training and building activities, and identification of problems once they occur. Mobility units will be better able to determine when demand will equal or exceed the supply of mission-days that they can provide if they develop and maintain an awareness of the supply of mission-days that they can sustain over the next several months. At the MAJCOM level, better forecasting of mission-day supply will allow better force management, allowing AMC to shift taskings from overstressed units to those in better shape.

The mission-day metric can also help the MAF to better schedule periodic training and upgrade events. Ideally, training could be fine-tuned to help units fill mission-day gaps by not sending pilots to training during times of high demand. Training could be completed during periods of relative calm.

Finally, the mission-day metric can help the MAF to identify specific problems and evaluate potential solutions. For example, during contingencies, the MAF has been tasked with flying more hours than it can sustain indefinitely, and between contingencies the MAF has been given too few hours to sustain needed training. The mission-day metric can help the MAF identify when it may need to increase or decrease the use of guard and reserve units and commercial cargo carriers. In addition, monitoring mission-days can help the MAF to monitor the variances in the supply and demand of mission-days. This support should help the MAF to determine the amount of flexibility that it should build into training schedules, its ability to use guard and reserve forces, and the contracts through which it buys commercial expansion time.

The mission-day metric could also help the Air Force determine the effects of special events on MAF flying demands. For example, the rotation of units out of and into Iraq or periodic Air Expeditionary Force rotations will place sizable demands upon the MAF. These demands can be compared with the supply of mission-days that the MAF can provide. The mission-day metric may have applicability to the combat air forces as well.

6. Conclusions

To date, there has not been a good metric that quantifies the ability of the MAF to conduct operations, train its personnel, and maintain readiness for future operations. Such a metric would also help to detect and identify the workload and OPTEMPO stresses placed upon the MAF. Therefore, we developed the mission-day metric, which measures the availability of crewmembers to fly, train, and continue their other military activities. It is essentially a person-day analysis of the activity required to conduct operations and stay ready for war.

In this study, we have described how we developed this metric. We applied it to an exemplar airlift wing, and we discussed how it might be used by the Air Force to plan operations at the MAJCOM and unit levels and to identify OPTEMPO problems.

Appendix

C-17 Pilot Count

Figure A.1 shows the number of C-17 pilots authorized and assigned in AMC from 1999 to 2003. The totals include all co-pilots, first pilots, aircraft commanders, instructor pilots, and flight-examiner pilots in AMC assigned to the 437th Airlift Wing, the 62nd Airlift Wing, the training units at Altus Air Force Base, and to other duties within AMC.

The numbers of both authorized and assigned C-17 pilots have grown as the number of C-17 aircraft operated by AMC has increased and a second operational wing (the 62nd Airlift Wing) was built. In 1999, the C-17 units were overmanned in anticipation of the arrival of additional aircraft and the need for experienced pilots to build a second C-17 wing. Growth in assigned C-17 pilots has lagged the growth in authorized pilots, resulting in an overall manning level of 75 percent for the C-17 by 2003.

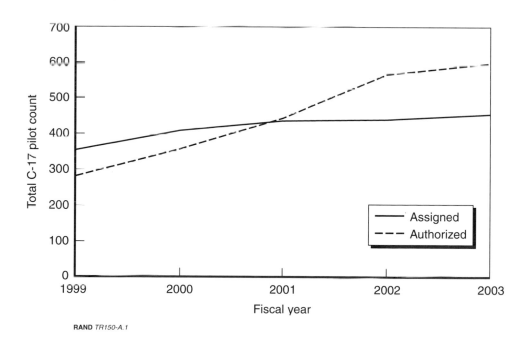

RAND *TR150-A.1*

Figure A.1—Total C-17 Pilot Count

A breakout of C-17 pilot numbers by unit is provided in Figure A.2. The C-17 pilots assigned to training units at Altus, as well as C-17 pilots assigned other duties within AMC, are included in the graphs labeled "Other AMC".

The 437th Airlift Wing held most of the assigned C-17 pilots in 1999. Gradually, the number of pilots in the 437th Wing declined as the numbers assigned to the 62nd Wing increased.

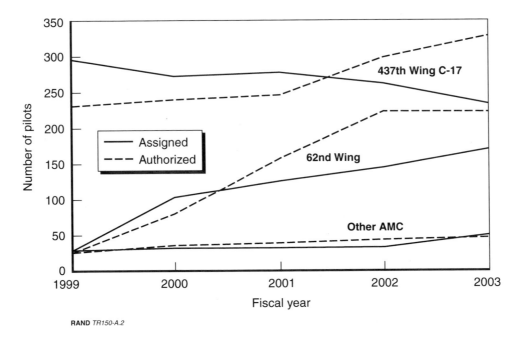

RAND *TR150-A.2*

Figure A.2—Authorized C-17 Pilot Count by Unit

Bibliography

Air Mobility Command, Mobility Force Management, AMC Instruction 11-206, *Flying Operations*, 1 June 1999.

Air Mobility Command (AMC/DOY), Contract Airlift Office, Operations Directorate, *Monthly Data (Carrier Detail) of International Airlift Contracts for FY2001 and FY2002* (as of 2/28/02).

Air Mobility Command Tanker Airlift Control Center, Global Reach For America, *Channel Performance and Analysis Report, FY02 Second Quarter*, 1 January 2002–31 March 2002.

Air Mobility Command Tanker Airlift Control Center, Global Reach For America, *Channel Performance and Analysis Report, FY02 First Quarter*, 1 October 2001–December 2001.

Air Mobility Command Tanker Airlift Control Center, Global Reach For America, *Channel Performance and Analysis Report, FY01 Second Quarter*, 1 January 2001–31 March 2001.

Air Mobility Command Tanker Airlift Control Center, Global Reach For America, *Channel Performance and Analysis Report, FY01 First Quarter*, 1 October 2000–31 December 2000.

Chow, Brian, Greg Jones, and Brent Thomas, *Designing Transload Concepts of Operations for the Civil Reserve Air Fleet to Respond to North Korean Chemical and Biological Threats*, Santa Monica, CA: RAND Corporation, MR-1301-AF, 2002 (Government publication; not for public release).

Chow, Brian, *The Peacetime Tempo of Air Mobility Operations: Meeting Demand and Maintaining Readiness*, Santa Monica, CA: RAND Corporation, MR-1506-AF, 2003.

Hamilton, Charles H., and Louis M. Datko, *Report on Career Decisions in the Air Force—Results of the 2000 USAF Careers and New Directions Surveys*, Air Force Personnel Center, Survey, November 2000.

Secretary of the Air Force, Air Force Instruction 11-2C-17, Vol. 1, *Flying Operations—C-17 Aircrew Training*, 1 February 1999.

Secretary of the Air Force, Air Force Instruction 11-2C-5, Vol. 1, *Flying Operations—C-5 Aircrew Training*, 1 January 1999.

Secretary of the Air Force, HQ AMC/DOTA, Air Force Instruction 11-2KC-135, Vol. 1, 1 January 1999.

Secretary of the Air Force, Air Force Instruction 11-2C-130, Vol. 1, *Flying Operations*, 1 November 1998.

Secretary of the Air Force, Air Force Instruction 11-2KC-135, Vol. 1, *Flying Operations*, 1 November 1998.